ideals®
MOTHER'S DAY

Within the corner of my heart
I've safely tucked away
A sweet bouquet of memories
From happy bygone days,
And there within each memory
I see your smiling face—
Dear Mother, you're a flower
That time will never fade.

—LOISE PINKERTON FRITZ

IDEALS PUBLICATIONS
NASHVILLE, TENNESSEE

Flowers for Mother
Georgia Sykes Sullivan

These velvet roses, fringed with Queen Anne's Lace,
Do they recall my first bouquet to you?
That ragged bunch of wilted dandelions
You treasured and arranged in your best vase?

The broken stems, the accidental weeds
I brought when I was small, received the care
Of lavish blooms in later years. It's true:
A mother's love is all a flower needs.

The Unexpected Gift
Georgia B. Adams

She stood there in the meadow
With a sweet bouquet:
Some yellow daisies that she'd plucked
While out to play.

Her eyes with merry twinkles danced
Out of the blue.
"I love you, Mommy dear," she said.
"These are for you!"

My heart welled up and over,
For a mite so small
Had given me her love . . . the gift
Greater than all!

A kiss, a hug, then off she went
On her merry way;
How did her young heart know that it
Was Mother's Day?

Spring and Mother

Caroline Darr Fitzsimmons

Far away in wooded fields,
'Neath the grass and mosses
Sleeping,
Nestling so still, so low,
Little heads are shyly peeping,
Waiting for the snows to go:
Violets, May-apple blossoms,
Forget-me-nots that you loved so.

They bring back childhood days to me;
School hours over, oft I
Gathered,
Mother, these sweet flowers for thee.
O'er hill and bank of stream I wandered;
To part from thee I never thought.
Dear to me are first spring blossoms,
Dear the precepts that you taught.

*The seasons come
And the seasons go
And many the
changes they bring,
But in the warmth
Of a mother's heart,
It is forever spring.*
—BARBARA BURROW

Rhododendrons in the Lady Bird Johnson Grove, Redwood National Park, California. Photograph by Carr Clifton

A Letter to My Mother

Joyce Carol Oates

Dear Mom,

I've meant so many times to tell you, and Daddy . . . how the human world divides into two: those who speak unhesitantly, smoothly saying I love you—and possibly not mean it; and those too shy or constrained by family custom or temperament to utter the words I love you—though they mean it. To the depths of what's called the soul.

How deep inside me, imprinted in infant memory, the sight of my young parents leaning over me, gazing at me smiling, lifting me in their arms. The wonder, the unspeakable mystery. Radiant unnamed faces of first love.

For this I've long believed: we carry our young parents within us, so much more vivid and alive, pulsing-alive, than any memory of ourselves as infants, children. We carry our young parents within us everywhere, through life. No wonder is ever quite equivalent to that first wonder. Blinking up from a crib, gaping in absolute trust and amazement lacking words to stammer, even to think, *Who are you? Why do you care for me? What does it mean, we are here together? Only hold me, hold me. Only feed me, love me, forever. . . .*

Always I've meant to tell you how in awe I am of the lives you and Daddy lived; your strength, your resilience, your good humor; your utter lack of self-pity; never complaining, except perhaps jokingly as if to indicate, *That's the way the world is, you might as well laugh. . . .*

In our old, precious snapshots, some of them a bit mangled, what an attractive young couple you are: you, with your bushy-springy hair and sweet smile, a look of girlish hope, openness; Daddy with his swarthy features, stiff-crested dark hair and heavy eyebrows, easy smile. Radiant faces of first love, romance. . . .

The house of my childhood is the house of recurring dreams yet subtly altered, the rooms mysterious, their dimensions uncertain; always there is a promise, alarming yet tantalizing, of rooms yet undiscovered, through a back wall, in the attic perhaps, or the cellar, rooms yet to be explored, beckoning. Your presence permeates the house, you are the house, its mysterious infinite rooms. You are the hazy light, the rich smell of damp earth, sunshine and grass, ripening pears. You are the humming buzzing not-quite-audible sound of fields, of distance. I see you pushing me on the swing, your hair reddish brown, you're wearing a shirt and pale blue "pedal pushers," I'm a lanky child of nine or ten on the swing Daddy made for me, the swing I loved, tough hemp rope hanging from a metal pipe secured between the branches of two tall trees in the backyard. I see you pushing me; I see myself stretching my legs upward, straining higher, higher, squealing with childish excitement, fearless, reckless, flying into the sky. So often I have wanted to tell you how, in patches of abrupt sunshine hundreds of miles and thousands of days from home, I am pulled back into that world as into the most seductive and most nourishing of dreams. I'm filled with a sense of wonder and awe and fear, regret for all that has passed, and for what must be surrendered, what we can imagine as life but cannot ever explain, cannot possibly put into words for all our effort, cannot utter aloud, dare not utter aloud, this succession of small particular moments like the movement of the red second hand on the General Electric clock, moments linked together as pearls are linked together to constitute a necklace, linked by tough, invisible string, the interior mystery. We were lucky, and we were happy, and I think we've always known.

Sometimes

Margaret E. Sangster

Sometimes I think God grew tired of making
Thunder and mountains and dawn redly breaking;
Weary of fashioning gorges and seas,
Weary of planting great forests of trees.
Sometimes I think God grew tired of heating
The earth with the sun and of fully completing
The whole of the world! God grew tired, and so
He took just a bit of the soft afterglow,
He took just a petal or two from a flower,
And took a songbird from a sweet-scented bower.
The dewdrops He took from the heart of a rose
And added the freshness of each breeze that blows.
Across long green meadows He took all the love
Left over from making His heaven above.
His kind fingers mixed them—God's hand and no other—
And made, for the first time, the soul of a mother.

Mother Love

Katherine Edelman

Such all-enduring faith and prayer,
Such sacrifice and tender care
Are woven through this love; it glows
With all the beauty of a rose.
Yet strong and firm as rock or tower,
It stands in dark or threatening hour.
A selfless love, that man reveres
With greater wonder through the years.

A Mother's Patience

Author Unknown

A fresh little bud in my garden,
With petals close folded from view,
Brightly nods me a cheery
    "Good morning"
Through the drops of a fresh bath
    of dew.

I must patiently wait its unfolding,
Though I long its full beauty to see;
Leave soft breezes and warm,
    tender sunshine
To perform the sweet office for me.

I may shield my fair baby blossom;
With trellis its weakness uphold;
With nourishment wisely sustain it
And cherish its pure heart of gold.

Then in good time, which
    is God's time,
Developed by sunshine and shower,
Some morning I'll find in the garden
Where my bud was,
    a beautiful flower.

So Lovingly Instilled

Lucile Waer

A gardener plants in the cool, sweet earth
Seeds and bulbs so small, so dry;
He dreams, as he gently tucks them there
Of the day they'll blossom and beautify
His garden, bringing vibrant colors for
All to see, rich perfume to fill the air.
No selfish gardener he: his hope, his wish
For all to love his garden sweet and fair.

A mother plants in a small child's heart
Love and kindness, precepts of truth, of good;
She instills by example, day by day,
Honor and tolerance of the brotherhood
Of all mankind. Her dream, her desire to
Someday see in her own fulfilled
And brought to blossom the beauty, the good
She so hopefully, so lovingly instilled.

Photograph by Jessie Walker

Maternal Song
Sudie Stuart Hager

How can I tell of a mother's worth?
By a song of the all-sustaining earth;
The earth that watches young plants rise
With arms outstretched to the distant skies.
The earth that gives them zeal to grow,
But keeps their eager roots in tow.
That urges them to stand up proud;
Sustains them when their heads are bowed;
And strengthens them to face again
The thrusts of wind and hail and rain,
So they may bloom, bear fruit and seed
To meet the hungering, tired world's need.
　　I sing of a kindly, nurturing earth
　　To tell of a mother's priceless worth.

My Mother's Garden
Jessie Goddard Broman

Today, in thinking, suddenly I knew
The secret of her garden and its ways,
Why all the curly roots made haste and grew
And were the first to start their blossom days.

Her pinks would hurry into spicy growing
While still the iris purpled lovely banners;
And past the time for poppies to be going,
The petals quite forgot their garden manners.

For I remember how she used to talk
To pansies that looked up with childlike faces;
She knelt to touch them by the garden walk,
And all their beauty took on added graces.

Now this one thing at last I surely know:
Flowers, like children, must have love to grow.

Because she is my mother, I so well understand
Why flowers bloom beneath the touch of her gentle hand.
—MARY RITA HURLEY

Photograph by Jane Grushow/
Grant Heilman Photography, Inc.

Sharing with God

James Keller

Every mother has the breathtaking privilege of sharing with God in the creation of new life. She helps bring into existence a soul that will endure for all eternity.

Every mother also has the unique honor of nurturing and developing the bit of the divine greatness in her child. Through her loving and devoted care, this youthful power can be directed from its earliest years to work for the glory of God and the benefit of others and, thus, contribute to its own temporal and eternal advantage.

Yes, a good mother can reach beyond the sanctuary of her home and help renew the face of the earth.

Faith

Virginia Scott Miner

We children turned to Mother
For her approving nod—
As sure of understanding
As when Mother turned to God.

Three Lovely Things

Grace V. Watkins

I saw three lovely things today,
Three lovely, silent things:
The soft white petals of a flower,
A soaring bird on wings
As blue as your eyes, and in the hour
Of dusk, my mother, I watched you pray.
I saw three lovely things today,
Three lovely, silent things.

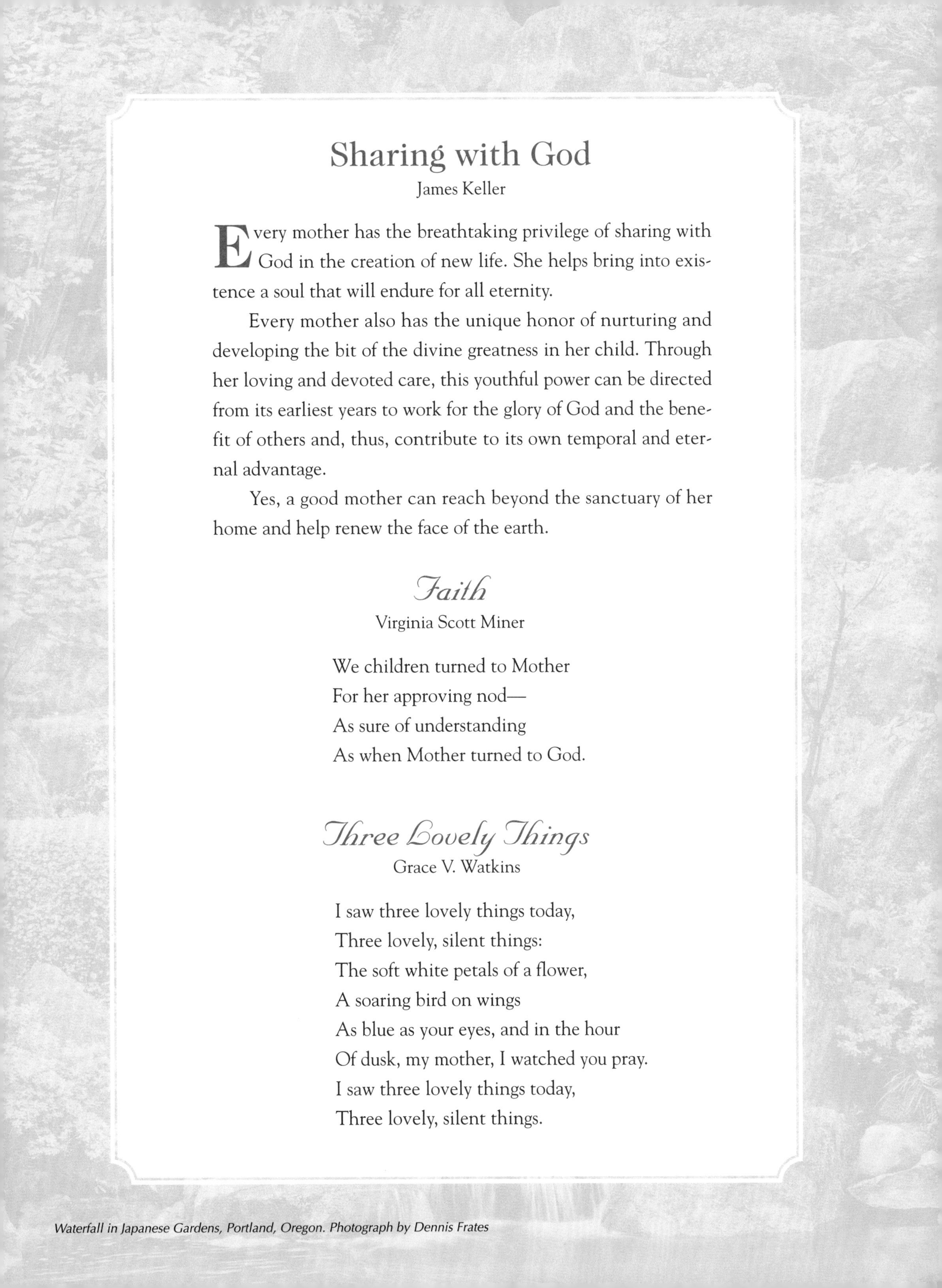

Waterfall in Japanese Gardens, Portland, Oregon. Photograph by Dennis Frates

My Best Friend

Elizabeth Dole

Mother is my best friend. She has been front and center in my life every step of the way. When I was a young girl, she was there to urge me to do my best. . . . And when the little scrapes and defeats of childhood occurred, Mother was there to turn my sorrows into smiles. . . .

One of the most vivid memories I have of her is on her knees, praying for me, others, and the needs of the world. When I go home to visit, I sleep in the same room with her because we love to talk to each other until we fall asleep.

Mother is unselfish, constantly thinking of others. She endears herself to people because she genuinely cares about every person who crosses her path.

Photograph by age fotostock/SuperStock

In Retrospect
Gretchen Gerhard

Among the finest things I know
Are hedges where wild roses grow;
The soft, returning green of spring;
Words carved within my wedding ring;
The frost etched on my windowpane;
The clean, sweet smell of summer rain.
Yet over these and what comes after,
I hold most dear my children's laughter.

The Little Things
Anne Campbell

It would be a weary world,
  God knows,
Without the little things!
The little stem that holds the rose,
The little bird that sings,
The little love that grows
  and grows,
The little thought that wings!

It would be a dreary world,
  God knows,
Without the little things!
The little joys, the little woes
That all our loving brings,
The little prayer at
  evening's close,
The little hand that clings!

Photograph by William H. Johnson

The Afterglow Means Hope

Marjorie Holmes

My mother always loved sunsets. This is true of many people, but Mother had a special feeling for them; she kept almost daily appointment with them, and she savored them until the last glow faded from the sky.

We lived in a small Iowa town which boasts a long and lovely lake. And though our house was small, it overlooked a tag end of the water where the sun seemed to fling its gaudiest banners at the end of the day.

"Oh, just look at that sunset!" Mother was always urging. "You can do those dishes later—your lessons can wait." We must stop whatever we were doing to follow her pleased gaze upward. "Isn't that the most beautiful sky you've ever seen?"

She always acted as if a sunset were something new and glorious and amazing, and we must observe it with as much intensity as if no sunset were ever to appear again. And though we often teased her about it, I realize now that those flaming sunsets compensated for many things we lacked during those grim, depressing years. They were her daily luxury.

Later, when the bright hues had melted into the dusk and there was nothing left of the sunset but a last lingering band of burning rose, she would return to the porch a minute and stand there, arms sometimes wrapped in her apron against the chill, and murmur: "The afterglow means hope."

Hope. The afterglow means—hope! The boy of your dreams would call. . . . The test grade would be high. . . . You'd get that scholarship for college. . . . The job you wanted so desperately would materialize. . . . The great, big, wonderful world of love and wealth and achievement would open up to you. . . . These are the faces of hope when you are young and looking up, eagerly seeking answers in a band of final color across a darkening sky.

As for her, dimly I sensed the meaning of hope to my mother: The problems of all those about her would be resolved. . . . Wounds would be healed, family frictions smoothed. . . . The

Wildflowers at sunset on Mount Rainier, Washington. Photograph by age fotostock/SuperStock

doctor's report on Dad would be favorable. . . . The company policy would be more generous. There would be enough money to go around. . . . Her children's often turbulent lives would get straightened out—the boys would find themselves, the girls would marry the right sweethearts—in time they would all be happy and make good.

For while the hooks upon which a youngster hangs his hopes are intensely selfish and personal, those of a mother are multiple; they encompass the entire circle of her family. Her dreams are no longer rooted in self, but in these others.

Yet standing on that porch together long ago, each of us saw in that smoldering band of light a symbol of happier, brighter tomorrows.

Hope. "The afterglow means hope." I don't know whether she had heard the phrase or coined it out of her own indomitable spirit. But I think of it whenever I see the quiet rosy afterlight that follows the blazing sunset. As if a few stubborn coals remain against the coming darkness, little fires of faith that cling long after the sunset is gone.

My Mother

Delphia M. Stubbs

You taught me to listen
For songs without words,
The lilt of the wind,
And trill of the birds.

You told me of wonders
That God will disclose
In the heart of a lily
And the face of a rose.

You taught me that stars
Are jewels of light,
That truth will endure
Approving the right.

From your beacon of light
A gleam I now borrow
For beautiful thinking
To brighten tomorrow.

My Legacy

Joyce E. Driver

She gave to me so many things:
A love of earth and sea,
A tenderness for creatures small,
The wind's wild melody.

There is laughter in a pansy's face,
Grandeur in a tree,
Radiance in the autumn leaves;
These things she showed to me.

We shared our joy of country lanes;
And, oh, she made me see
The very best that life can hold
Is absolutely free.

She said, "Be still at eventide,
At the close of a lovely day,
And watch the gentle cloak of night
Erase the sun's last ray."

Though life sometimes grows hectic
Like a wild and stormy sea,
I do not fear because I have
My mother's legacy.

Yaquina Lighthouse, Oregon. Photograph by Dennis Frates

What Mother Loves

Alice Leedy Mason

A mother loves
The gentle breeze
That whispers in
The willow trees.
She loves the hills,
The winding path,
And hearing little
Children laugh.

A mother loves
All newborn things—
The colt, the pup;
Their presence brings
An understanding,
Tenderness,
And hands that touch
With gentleness.

A mother loves
The quiet time,
Books to share
In prose and rhyme,
Kittens chasing
Butterflies,
And clouds that clutter up
The skies.

These are the things
That make life real;
The sound of bells,
How strangers feel,
A deer in flight,
The wild bird's call—
A mother knows
And loves them all.

Defeat

Barbara A. Jones

I know the puppy's very new,
And I know that he's lonely too—
But puppy's place is in the shed,
And not with you, deep down in bed.
Tears will not move me—not at all,
Not even though he's soft and small
And knows you when you come from play;
The shed's his place and there he'll stay,
    because—
Yes, he has lovely soft, big paws,
And yes, I love his ears that flop. . . .
Now, mind: not underneath! On top.

Photograph by Mark Raycroft/Minden Pictures

The Mailbox

Patty Duncan

You're a wonderful mother," I wrote on the Mother's Day card with the picture of sunflowers, garden gloves, and watering can. "You were always home for me after school, with warm cookies and milk. You led our 4-H club and worked in PTA. Best of all, now you're my friend, sharing with me a love of beauty, puzzlement at the mysteries of men, and respect for children."

I walked out the gravel driveway to the mailbox, opened the metal door, and slid in the card. As I shut the door and pulled up the red flag, I remembered another mailbox from long ago. . . .

As a child, I spent hours in a small playhouse in the backyard. I decked it out with curtains strung on twine, a window box planted with marigolds, and a mailbox made from a coffee can.

The can was painted with green house paint and fitted with a small board inside to create a flat horizontal surface. It was nailed to the outside wall of the playhouse, next to the window.

One languid summer day, I ran into the house and found my mother mopping the kitchen floor.

"Mama," I asked, "could you bring me some mail?"

She straightened up and held the mop in one hand, massaging the small of her back with the other. She smiled, and her eyes softened as she looked at me, her suntanned, pigtailed sprite.

"Well, yes, I think I can, after I finish this floor," she said. "You go back to the playhouse and wait awhile. I'll be there."

So I ran outside, letting the screen door slam behind me. I skipped down the narrow brick path to the clothesline and under it to the playhouse beside the dwarf apple tree. I busied myself with little-girl housekeeping: washing my doll dishes, tidying the bed, sweeping the floor with the toy cornstraw broom.

Then I heard steps on the brick path.

"Mail time," Mama called in a high voice. Then I heard the thunk of envelopes firmly striking the inside of the coffee can.

I waited to give her time to walk back to the house, then rushed out of the playhouse and reached into the can to grab my treasure. Shuffling through it, I found three envelopes, a catalog, and a small package. What a haul!

I sat on the grass that sloped down to the garden to open it.

Naturally, I went for the package first. Tearing away the brown grocery-sack paper, I lifted the lid from a tiny box. Wow! Two sticks of Juicy Fruit gum; a square of waxed paper wrapped around a handful of chocolate chips, raisins, and miniature marshmallows; and a new Pink Pearl eraser. I munched on the snack mixture while I explored the rest of my mail.

Thumbing through the seed catalog, I enjoyed the brightly colored flower pictures. Then I spread the envelopes out in my hand. Each was addressed to "Patty, Playhouse, Back Yard, Oregon" and posted with an S & H Green Stamp. I slipped my finger under the flap of one and ripped it open. It held a flyer from a car insurance company. In the next I found an advertisement for magazine subscriptions with a hundred

tiny stamps to stick onto the order form. From the last envelope, I pulled a page of notepaper.

"How are you doing?" I read in my mother's perfect printing. "It's beautiful weather here, though a little hot for me. I've been canning beans. We have a lovely, large garden, as usual. Do come visit us. You know you are always welcome. Love, Mama."

She signed it in "writing" with swirls at the beginning of the "M" and at the end of the "a."

That was probably forty years ago.

I thought Mama and I had become close friends only recently. But remembering the mailbox, I realized I was wrong. The mother who took the time from her mopping and canning to gather up some junk mail and trinkets to put into a package, write a personal note, and deliver it all in true play-acting style was my special companion even back then. Mama was always my friend.

When You Thought I Wasn't Looking

Mary Rita Schilke Korzan

When you thought I wasn't looking,
You hung my first painting on the refrigerator
And I wanted to paint another.

When you thought I wasn't looking,
You fed a stray cat
And I thought it was good to be
    kind to animals.

When you thought I wasn't looking,
You baked a birthday cake just for me
And I knew that little things
    were special things.

When you thought I wasn't looking,
You said a prayer
And I believed there was a God
    that I could always talk to.

When you thought I wasn't looking,
You kissed me good night
And I felt loved.

When you thought I wasn't looking,
I saw tears come from your eyes
And I learned that sometimes
        things hurt—
But that it's all right to cry.

When you thought I wasn't looking,
You smiled
And it made me want to
    look that pretty too.

When you thought I wasn't looking,
You cared
And I wanted to be everything I could be.

When you thought I wasn't looking,
I looked . . .
And wanted to say thanks
For all those things you did
When you thought I wasn't looking.

The Nicest Thing My Mother Ever Said to Me

Marilyn Pribus

Once, when I was about twelve, my mother and I were talking. Perhaps we were doing the dishes or coming home from the dentist—I don't recall exactly—but she was recounting some clever thing I did when I was three. Her memories, edited by the years, pictured me as a perfect preschooler. I compared myself unfavorably with the golden-haired charmer in the photo album. There I was at twelve—awkward and bespectacled with my hair frizzed from home permanents. (Frizz was not the style then.) Other girls got lots more valentines in the decorated box at school, and my bosom friends were all imaginary. "When was I the best age?" I asked a trifle hesitantly.

Mother looked at me in surprise. "Right now," she told me. "You're the best age you've ever been right now."

I was about twenty-one when she came to my college for the annual Mothers' Weekend. At a luncheon we were talking about how fast time flies—it seemed only last month she was a Brownie leader and I was a Brownie. Now I had almost graduated from college. I wasn't a cheerleader, and although my grades were good, I knew deep down that they could have been better. Hairstyles were now bouffant, but my hair was in a long ponytail, and a skinny ponytail at that. There were lots of Saturday nights I'd be at the dorm desk ringing the rooms of other girls as their dates arrived for a dance or a movie. I had no firm plans for a career, and no applications filed for graduate school or the Peace Corps. I commented to my mother that I supposed she missed her "little girl."

"Heavens, no," she said emphatically. "You're the best age now you've ever been."

By age twenty-four, I was married to my high school sweetheart and had two babies. Suddenly, I found myself and our two boys living in the spare bedroom at my parents' home. My husband had been transferred to the Air Force base in Okinawa, and it would be three months before we could join him. There I was back at home, but this time with that unmistakable aura of diapers, orange juice, and baby powder. Coping with infants who awakened at dawn, refused their oatmeal, then nibbled on the newspapers, I was turning my mother's well-ordered home into a nursery. I ate a bit too much, slept a bit too much, and crabbed a bit too much.

Apologetically I told my mother I was sure she'd be glad to get back to normal—that the kids were fun for a while but I was rather too old to be her child. "Oh, no," she said. "I enjoy the boys just as I enjoyed you as a baby, but right now you are the best age you've ever been."

Last fall I turned forty. My "babies" are teenagers with vacuum-cleaner appetites and they love to point out that at "only" five foot seven I'm the family midget. My house is never entirely clean; I'm inclined to start planning dinner at quarter to five. And although frizz is now in style, my hair is straight as a string. Nevertheless, during Christmas vacation when my folks flew from New York to visit, my mother told me I'm the best age ever.

Last week, my son and I were having a somewhat heated discussion, although I've entirely forgotten the subject. We often have somewhat heated discussions on a variety of topics: we hold vastly differing views on the socially redeeming value of television, a suitable time to be in on Saturday night, what constitutes a clean room, who should haul out the garbage cans on rainy Wednesday mornings, and whether a just-under-a-quarter-full gas tank is pretty empty or has quite a bit left.

"Boy," he finally said in exasperation. "I bet you wish I was four years old again and just did what you wanted."

But looking up at him I thought for only a moment before saying honestly, "No, Son, that's not true. Right now you are the best age you've ever been."

And with those words I offered to him a gift of total acceptance, a feeling of worth and worthiness and security, a sense of value and confidence and self-esteem. I passed on my mother's gift of love.

My Mother's Recipe
Edna Moore Schultz

While rummaging the other day,
I found a treasure tucked away.
It was a faded recipe
My mother once had given me.
I still recall my great delight
When eating every luscious bite
Of that grand cake of long ago—
None other can compare, I know.
I thought, "I'll give my folks a treat
With something really good to eat."

I hoped that I could truly bake
My mother's special chocolate cake.
But then I read the recipe,
And more and more it stymied me!
"Take lots of flour," the paper said,
"The kind you use for making bread.
A scoop of sugar should be fine,
And with some butter then combine.
A dash of salt is all you need.
Just stir with ordinary speed.

"Drop in an egg—or maybe two.
Pour in vanilla like I do.
Add milk until you've the right touch—
Put in enough, but not too much.
The chocolate's better with milk sour;
Then bake for very near an hour."
Ah me, I'd love to bake that cake
Again for my dear family's sake,
But I think Mother gave to me
A puzzle, not a recipe.

Photograph by Jessie Walker

Confession
Lalia Mitchell Thornton

I should like cleanness, neatness, order,
A box hedge and a well-kept border,
Slim maids in aprons spotless white,
And prism chandeliers at night;
But there is something in me calls
For mud-tracked steps and toy-strewn halls,
For sticky fingers on the pane,
And childish faces tanned and plain.

I should like smugness, books and pictures,
High walls and heavy ornate fixtures,
A straightened desk, a quiet room,
An air austere, a cloistral gloom;
But there is something in me needs
A tangled garden, flowers and weeds,
The touch of clinging little hands—
These are the things my soul demands.

Time Out
Kay Andrews

When the oatmeal is finished
And wiped off their faces,
The boxes of lunches
Are snatched from their places,
The sound of the school bus
Makes feet fly and scurry,
And Mother is kissed
(Or missed) in the hurry,
Then . . .

I reheat the coffee
And fill up my cup
And, ignoring the mess,
Pick the newspaper up;
I settle me back,
Put my cares on the shelf,
And take ten lovely minutes
All to myself.

Photograph by Larry Lefever/Grant Heilman Photography, Inc.

A Perfect Mother

Pamela Kennedy

I wonder if every kid in the world at some time has not wished for a different mother. Not just any old mother, but the perfect mother! Most of the mothers I know have heard about this woman. We've never actually seen her; sharing our accumulated insights, I think we have a pretty good idea of what she is like.

She is not too old and not too young. In other words, she's old enough to know all the stuff you need to know to be a mother, but young enough to wear pretty clothes, have a hairdo that isn't dumb-looking, and keep up with all the kids' activities. She has a great imagination because she must think of interesting activities when "there's nothing to do," make a complete dinner when someone "forgot" to pick up the groceries, and create an Indian costume in one hour.

She drives like a Formula One race car driver because her children do not tell her they must go somewhere until it is almost too late to get there. But she is always patient, even under the worst circumstances, knowing that if she loses her temper or uses profanity, her words will be quoted all over the neighborhood by her adoring children.

This paragon of motherhood has an amazingly long attention span, allowing her to sit through thousands of hours of ballet practice, baseball games, piano lessons, and karate classes without complaint. While she waits, she creates flawless counted cross-stitch panoramas and needlepoint pillows to give to her fortunate relatives at Christmas. She does not waste time or fritter away her leisure with pointless activities like bridge, or golf, or reading. Instead, her free time is full of fascinating hobbies like ironing, running errands, supervising Brownie campouts, and picking up last-minute items for the school party.

Other children, with less-than-perfect mothers, flock to her house, where it is always fun! She has cookies and sodas tumbling from her cupboards in great abundance which she allows her own children, and any others around the house, to eat, mostly between meals. And when she fixes dinner she sticks to pizza, burgers, and fried chicken and never ventures into exotic fare like quiche or any dish featuring broccoli.

Children living at the perfect mother's house do not have to pick up their rooms, take out the trash, eat their veggies, or go to bed at any particular time. They may chew with their mouths open, put both elbows on the table, and belch with impunity. They never have to watch the news, documentaries, or "Wall Street Week," but are permitted to gaze at cartoons and situation comedies until their eyes cross.

When the perfect mother takes her children shopping at the mall, she never acts like she knows them. She walks at least ten feet behind them unless they are at the cash register and need money to pay for their purchases. She refrains

Photograph by Gary Moss/Botanica/Jupiter Images

from offering opinions on her children's choices and never, never says any of the following things:

"I wouldn't let you go out of the house in that!"

"We are not going to pay twice as much for those just because they have an Italian name stitched on the back pocket!"

"Do you think money grows on trees?"

"When I was your age . . ."

She is always delighted to have any of her children's friends over to spend the night and never threatens to call their parents if they get too loud at three AM. In the morning she is cheerful as, without a murmur, she wades through scattered popcorn and sleeping bags on her way to fix pancakes for her grumpy guests.

When there is a school program, she always shows up but sits in the back so her children will not be embarrassed by her presence. She does not applaud too loudly, but recalls in vivid detail every moment of her child's performance so she can respond appropriately when interrogated later.

In short, the perfect mother does everything her child believes she ought. But we less-than-perfect mothers must carry on, making the same kind of statements our own mothers made, hearing our children make the same kind of complaints we made, and reassuring them, as we were once reassured: "Honey, when you have kids of your own, you can be the first perfect mother!"

The Family Wash-Line

Mrs. Roy L. Peifer

Upon a backyard wash-line,
In message bright and bold,
The story of a happy home
And family is told.

Time was, when we first married,
When days were bright and blue,
Our wash-line told a story
Of home, dear, just for two.

I hung them out,
    your clothes and mine,
But at the end of year
White squares proclaimed
    the message:
"A baby's living here."

Do you recall, one morning
When all was bright and fine,
You touched the little dresses
Swaying on the line,

And then, dear, in a whisper—
Perhaps more like a prayer—
You wished for little overalls
To swing beside them there?

Then pretty soon,
    to bless our hearts,
Our dear boy came along,
And once again
    the wash-lines hummed
Their lullaby of song.

For then the little overalls,
Much to our heartfelt joy,
Proclaimed to all
    the passing world,
"Here lives a little boy!"

And so upon the wash-line,
For all the world to see
Was told the precious story
Of home and family.

Wash Day

Alma Robison Higbee

Mark this as drudgery if you will, but I
Love the sudsy scent and the rhythmic tune
Of busyness; I love the rinsing in liquid sky
Of these familiar garments, then soon
I hang them up, dress, pillowcase and sheet,
Shirt and overalls, securely pinned
To catch and hold the clover scent and sweet,
Clean fragrance borrowed from sun and wind.

Cleaning Day

Anne Campbell

It is a way of praying,
To bend above unsightly floors and sweep;
To wash soiled walls; to scrub a porch; to keep
A little dwelling spotless; to align
Oneself with all the cleanliness and order
Of God's orderly world. Clean clothes are swaying
In the warm, Maytime breeze. The air is sweet
With blossoms planted in the yard's green border.
It is a way of praying,
To keep a house fragrant and neat!

Photograph by Jessie Walker

Photograph by Jessie Walker

My Mother
Barbara Bush

My mother was a striking beauty who left the world a more beautiful place than she found it. She grew lovely flowers, did the finest needlepoint I have ever seen, and knew how to keep an exquisite home.

I understand her better now than I did then. I certainly did not appreciate all the pressures she must have felt until I also became a mother. She taught me a great deal, although neither of us realized it at the time. Probably her most important lesson was an inadvertent one. You have two choices in life: you can like what you do, or you can dislike it. I have chosen to like it.

My memory of her is of someone always marvelously fresh and pretty, although when I examine it, I see that she wore the same dresses year after year. But she could twist a ribbon in such a way or so pin a flower at her throat that she looked as though she wore a new gown.

—Pearl S. Buck

Embroideries

Kari Sharp Hill

In the linen closet, next to the cheerful prints and modern geometrics, lie a pair of hand-embroidered pillowcases. My mother stitched them, this particular pair, when I was nine years old.

Her skilled hands fed the needle through the stiff new fabric, creating a border of blue-birds using their gentle beaks to twist and wrap yellow ribbons into plump bows.

Often I begged her to let me try. She would smile and pull my eternal dresser scarf from her basket. With uncooperative fingers, I struggled. The thread would tangle. There would be gaping holes where French knots would have rested. I fussed until my project was returned to the sanctuary of Mom's sewing basket.

"That's enough for now," she would say. "Go enjoy the fresh air—it may rain tomorrow." I'd run outside, graciously released from my defeat.

I was fifteen the first time a boy broke my heart. I came home, dropped my coat on the sofa, and ran into my room. I crossed his name out in my diary with a black magic marker. I cried and decided to rededicate myself to becoming a famous writer. I'd make that boy pay the price of being a villain many times over in my novels.

When I came out of my room, red-eyed and resolved, I found my mother on her favorite end of the sofa stitching. The TV tray next to her offered two glasses of ice and a rare bottle of Coca-Cola.

We drank the pop while mom worked on another pair of pillowslips. "Mom, I'm going to be a writer," I said.

"A writer." She tried it on her tongue the way girls try out their boyfriends' last names attached to their own first names. "A writer needs a good hat." She smiled.

"What kind of hat?"

She started stitching again. "A big hat with lots of fruit or flowers on it, something you'd never wear in public, a hat to wear when you're thinking up stories in your room." She glanced up, punctuated the air with her needle. "My Aunt Sally had a hat like that. She wrote novels."

This was the first I'd heard of Aunt Sally, a possible genetic benefactor of my writing abilities. The afternoon passed with wonderful stories about her and the crazy things she did.

"She never married," Mom said. "She was a heartbreaker." I decided I'd be a heartbreaker too.

Once, home from college on spring break, I found Mom working on a tablecloth for my hope chest. I told her I'd never get married.

"I have many hopes for you," she said.

My mother never kept any of her own embroidery—she gave it as gifts, donated to bazaars. All my friends' babies got embroidered quilts and baby-size pillows with matching cases.

"Who is that for?" I'd ask when she

Photograph by Jessie Walker

started something new. "For your aunt," she'd say, or, "Emma's granddaughter is getting married."

"Why don't you do something for yourself?" I asked once. "You've given away so much."

She looked up, surprised. "I've done them all for myself. Every piece I've ever done has been stitched with conversations or dreams, thoughts about Brazil and women's lib. And worries." She grinned. "The day you told me you'd be a writer, my work saved me. I heard you crying in your room, and I had an idea some boy had caused it. I didn't know what to do." My mother laughed, remembering.

"So you poured us a Coke."

"And I made up some crazy stories about your Aunt Sally."

"You made them up?" I couldn't believe it. "I loved those stories. I even bought a hat. I put so much fake fruit on it, it kept slipping down over my eyes when I typed."

"I know," she said. "Remember those placemats I made your cousin Marjorie for her bridal shower?"

"The ones with the cantaloupe and kiwi and bananas and stuff all over them."

My mother nodded. "I made that set in honor of some of your finest hours at the typewriter."

I'm giving my mother a cross-stitched picture for Mother's Day—it's a picture of a mother and child reading. I stitched in some thoughts, my love, careful prayers, memories, and time.

Though there are certain qualities of permanence woven into my mother's linens, the truly lasting craft will be my mother's love embroidered across my heart.

Little Rocking Chair
Laura W. Stevens

You're just a little rocking chair
Of reed and painted white,
So low and stout and comfy
For lullabies at night.

'Twas many, many years ago,
When you were fresh and new,
That Grandma rocked her little ones
To slumberland with you;

Then as the years passed quickly by,
The same endearing sight

As Mother cradled her babies
And gently held them tight.

Next came my turn to know the joy
Of that eternal bliss,
To soothe the cares of my baby dear
And leave her with a kiss.

Now soon again, little rocking chair,
Love's sweetest story you'll tell,
As Janet rocks her little one
And prays all will be well.

My Mother's Rocking Chair
Marcella Drennan Malarky

I loved my mother's rocking chair,
So cheery and so bright;
'Twas small and round and painted red;
It was my chief delight.

The seat was deep, the back was round,
It fit you oh-so-snug;
I loved to rock in mother's arms,
She'd hold me tight and hug
Me oh-so-close up to her heart;
Then all my fears would soon depart.

I would love to see once more, my dear,
That lovely rocking chair,
To be a child in mother's arms,
To feel the comfort there.

And that old kitchen, the old blue clock,
The winding wooden stair,
But memory now has painted clear
A picture oh-so-fair
Of Mother and her kitchen and
The little rocking chair.

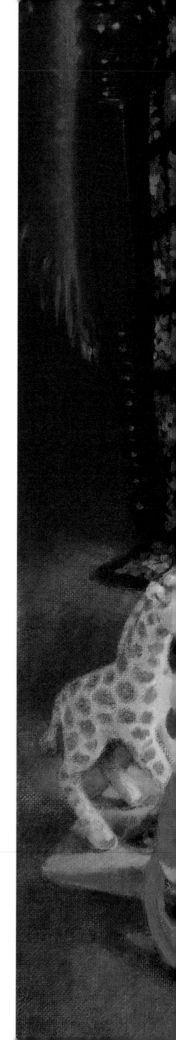

Mothering

Catherine Calvert

We came from a long line of doll lovers: my grandmother still had her china-headed doll, the star of Christmas 1902, tucked in a drawer; and the only time I saw my mother cry was when I dropped and broke her Bye-lo baby, the much-pined-for present of her seventh year. So we had families of dolls, platoons of dolls, sorted by size and type, and each with as emphatic a personality as our own. . . .

We mothered our dolls, as our mother mothered us, weaving her secure background for us as she worked just out of earshot, making something cinnamony, perhaps, or bent at her own sewing task, turning out another superior example of doll couture.

THE LORD'S BLESSING. *Painting by Kathy Lawrence. From the Visions of Faith Collection, courtesy of Mill Pond Press (www.millpond.com)*

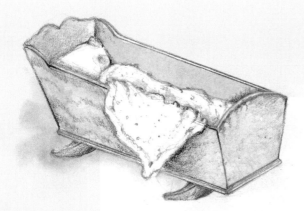

She Is the Song, I Am the Music

Sylvia Wave Carberry

As I soothe my child to sleep
those words you taught me long ago
come floating through my heart.
Softly I begin to sing
and in the silence of the night
become your instrument again.

Lullabies

Starrlette L. Howard

I've yet to meet the angels
That are in heaven's place,
But I've seen the glow of motherhood
And a fragile baby's face.
I'm sure there's more to measure
Than only gold could bring,
And I'm sure all heaven listens
To a mother when she sings.

Candlelight Is Lovelight
Thelma Scott Kiser

When the storm was raging
And the lights went out,
Mama lit a candle
And gathered us about.
Then she took
   Grimm's Fairy Tales
From the bookcase shelf,
And soon, instead
   of howling storm,
We listened to an elf
Or, *clip-clop*,
   Billy Goat Gruff
Instead of thunderclaps.
Instead of stark reality,
We shared a bright perhaps.

And as that flickering candle
Lit Mama's smiling face,
We children lost our fear
   of storms,
And wonder took its place.

Now when I see a candle,
I see my mother's smile;
Viewing that hypnotic flame,
I am a child awhile.
Yes, the light from any candle
Forms a circle drawing close
Those childhood scenes
   of home and love
And all I treasure most.

A Golden Memory
Johanna Ter Wee

Long years have passed, yet there remains
A memory forged with golden chains
That ever binds me to the past—
A childhood memory made to last.
For constantly throughout the years,
Remembrance comes of banished fears
When lamps were dimmed and prayers were said
And Mother tucked me into bed.

Photograph by Jessie Walker

Mama's Room
Carol Bessent Hayman

Mama's room was the big front bedroom just to the left as you entered the two-story frame house with its sprawling porches on three sides, upstairs and down. Somehow we always gravitated to her room, and it became more living room to us than the parlor across the hall or the dining room with its wrought-iron day bed behind the parlor.

Each morning, Mama fluffed her big feather bed—the focal point of the room—into a cloudy mass and topped it with two snowy white feather pillows. Mama was very particular about her bed. You did not sit or loll about on it; and it was a treat of treats to get to sleep in this confection, which always felt just as good as it looked.

An assortment of furniture clustered around the bed, but I remember best Mama's dresser, which held her comb, brush, and mirror and an array of perfume and cologne bottles. If Mama had a weakness, it was for smelling good. "English Lavender" and "Evening in Paris" were her favorites, and each Christmas and birthday saw her stock replenished.

Several rocking chairs waited nearby, one of which we referred to as "Mama's chair"; and when the day's work ended and she could rest, we always knew we could find her here. It was here that I came with my confidences and my problems, and it was here that I brought my little joys and sorrows; for nothing seemed complete until it had been shared with Mama. She always listened as if each word I said had importance, and her opinion was always wise and full of love for me.

Photograph by Jessie Walker

The Perfect Mother

Pearl S. Buck

Never was a woman more richly mother than this woman, bubbling over with a hundred little songs and scraps of gay nonsense to beguile a child from tears. . . . Her hands were swift to tenderness and care and quiet brooding tending when need arose. Never was she a more perfect mother than during the summers on the mountaintop when she could give herself freely to her children. She led them here and there in search of beauty, and she taught them how to love cliffs and rugged rocks outlined against the sky, and to love also little dells where ferns and moss grow about a pool. Beauty she brought into her house, too, and filled the rooms with ferns and flowers.

Photograph by Terry Donnelly/Donnelly Austin Photography

A Mother's Picture
Alice Cary

A lady, the loveliest ever the sun looked
    down upon,
You must paint for me.
Oh, if I could only make you see
The clear blue eyes, the tender smile,
The sovereign sweetness, the gentle grace,
The woman's soul, and the angel's face
That are beaming on me all the while—
But I need not speak these foolish words;
One word tells you all I would say,
She is my mother; and you will agree
That all the rest may be thrown away.

The Picture
William Jennings Bryan

The painter has with his brush transferred the landscape to the canvas with such fidelity that the trees and grasses seem almost real; he has made even the face of a maiden seem instinct with life; but there is one picture so beautiful that no painter has ever been able to perfectly reproduce it, and that is the picture of the mother holding in her arms her babe.

Photograph by Nancy Matthews

Thank You, God,
For pretending not to notice that one of
Your angels is missing and for guiding her to me.
You must have known how much I would need her, so
You turned Your head for a minute and allowed
her to slip away to me.
Sometimes I wonder what special name You had for her.
I call her "Mother."

—BERNICE MADDUX

Definition
Grace Noll Crowell

I search among the plain and lovely words

To find what the one word *Mother* means; as well

Try to define the tangled song of birds,

The echo in the hills of one clear bell.

One cannot snare the wind, or catch the wings

Of shadows flying low across the wheat;

Ah, who can prison simple, natural things

That make the long days beautiful and sweet?

Mother—a word that holds the tender spell

Of all the dear essential things of earth;

A home, clean sunlit rooms, the good smell

Of bread, a table spread, a glowing hearth,

And love beyond the dream of anyone. . . .

I search for words for her . . . and there are none.

Photograph by Jessie Walker

My Mother
Frederic H. Adams

She was as good as goodness is;
Her acts and all her words were kind,
And high above all memories
I hold the beauty of her mind.

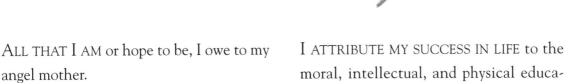

ALL THAT I AM or hope to be, I owe to my angel mother.

—Abraham Lincoln

I ATTRIBUTE MY SUCCESS IN LIFE to the moral, intellectual, and physical education which I received from my mother.

—George Washington

The love of a mother is never exhausted.
It never changes, it never tires.
It endures through all; in good repute, in bad repute,
    and in the face of the world's condemnation,
A mother's love still lives on.

—WASHINGTON IRVING

MY MOTHER WAS THE MAKING OF ME. She was so true, so sure of me, and I felt that I had someone to live for, someone I must not disappoint.

—Thomas Edison

WHEN GOD THOUGHT of mother, He must have laughed with satisfaction and framed it quickly—so rich, so deep, so divine, so full of soul, power, and beauty was the conception.

—Henry Ward Beecher

There Is No Job More Important than Parenting

Benjamin Carson

The simplest way to say it is this: I believe in my mother.

My belief began when I was just a kid. I dreamed of becoming a doctor.

My mother was a domestic. Through her work, she observed that successful people spent a lot more time reading than they did watching television. She announced that my brother and I could only watch two or three preselected television programs during the week. With our free time, we had to read two books each from the Detroit Public Library and submit to her written book reports. She would mark them up with check marks and highlights. Years later we realized her marks were a ruse. My mother was illiterate; she had only received a third-grade education.

Although we had no money, between the covers of those books I could go anywhere, do anything, and be anybody.

When I entered high school, I was an A student, but not for long. I wanted the fancy

---

*My first desire for knowledge
and my earliest passion
for reading were awakened
by my mother.*
—CHARLES DICKENS

---

clothes. I wanted to hang out with the guys. I went from being an A student to a B student to a C student, but I didn't care. I was getting the high fives and the low fives and the pats on the back. I was cool.

One night my mother came home from working her multiple jobs, and I complained about not having enough Italian knit shirts. She said, "Okay, I'll give you all the money I made this week scrubbing floors and cleaning bathrooms, and you can buy the family food and pay the bills. With everything left over, you can have all the Italian knit shirts you want."

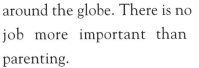

I was very pleased with that arrangement, but once I got through allocating money, there was nothing left. I realized my mother was a financial genius to be able to keep a roof over our heads and any kind of food on the table, much less buy clothes.

I also realized that immediate gratification wasn't going to get me anywhere. Success required intellectual preparation.

I went back to my studies and became an A student again, and eventually I fulfilled my dream and became a doctor.

Over the years my mother's steadfast faith in God has inspired me, particularly when I had to perform extremely difficult surgical procedures or when I found myself faced with my own medical scare. . . .

My story is really my mother's story—a woman with little formal education or worldly goods who used her position as a parent to change the lives of many people around the globe. There is no job more important than parenting.

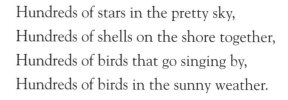

Only One Mother
Author Unknown

Hundreds of stars in the pretty sky,
Hundreds of shells on the shore together,
Hundreds of birds that go singing by,
Hundreds of birds in the sunny weather.

Hundreds of dewdrops to greet the dawn,
Hundreds of bees in the purple clover,
Hundreds of butterflies on the lawn,
But only one mother the wide world over.

ISBN-13: 978-0-8249-1314-4
ISBN-10: 0-8249-1314-0
Published by Ideals Publications, a Guideposts Company
535 Metroplex Drive, Suite 250, Nashville, Tennessee 37211
www.idealspublications.com

Publisher, Peggy Schaefer
Editor, Melinda Rathjen
Art Director, Marisa Calvin
Permissions, Lori Archer
Copy Editor, Kaye Dacus

Cover: Photograph by Al Riccio/Getty Images
Inside front cover: Painting by George Hinke
Inside back cover: Painting by Frances Hook

ACKNOWLEDGMENTS

BUCK, PEARL S. "The Perfect Mother" and "Mother's Hands" excerpted from *The Exile*. Copyright © 1936 by Pearl S. Buck. Published by Reynal & Hitchcock, Inc. Used by permission of Harold Ober Associates, Inc. BUSH, BARBARA. "My Mother" from *Barbara Bush: A Memoir*. Copyright © 1994 by Barbara Bush. Published by Scribner, a division of Simon & Schuster, Inc. CALVERT, CATHERINE. "Mothering" from *Dear Grandmother: Recollections of Love*. Copyright ©1998 by Hearst Books. Used by permission of Sterling Publishing. CARBERRY, SYLVIA WAVE. "She Is the Song, I Am the Music" from *Mothers and Daughters*, published 2001 by Harmony Books. Used by permission of the author. CARSON, BENJAMIN. "There Is No More Important Job Than Parenting" from *This I Believe*, published 2006 by Henry Holt. Used by permission of Benjamin S. Carson, Sr., M.D., Professor & Director of Pediatric Neurosurgery, Johns Hopkins Medical Institutions. CROWELL, GRACE NOLL. "Definition" from *Light of the Years*. Copyright © 1936 by Grace Noll Crowell. Published by Harper & Brothers Publishers. DOLE, ELIZABETH. "My Best Friend" excerpted from "Elizabeth Dole's Heart and Soul" by Julie A. Talerico from *Today's Christian Woman* magazine July/August 1993, published by Christianity Today, International, Carol Stream, IL. DUNCAN, PATTY. "The Mailbox" © 1997 by Patty Duncan, from *The Lookout*, May 11, 1997. Used by permission of the author. HAYMAN, CAROL BESSENT. "Mama's Room" from *These Lovely Days.*

Copyright © 1971 by Carol Bessent Hayman. Used by permission of the author. HOLMES, MARJORIE. "The Afterglow Means Hope" from *How Can I Find You God?* Copyright © 1967 by Marjorie Holmes. Used by permission of Dystel & Goderich Literary Management. KORZAN, MARY RITA SCHILKE. "When You Thought I Wasn't Looking" from *A Time to Care*. Copyright © 1989 by Mary Rita Schilke Korzan. Used by permission of the author. OATES, JOYCE CAROL. "A Letter to My Mother" from *The New York Times Magazine* 5/12/1996. Copyright © 1996 Ontario Review. Used by permission of John Hawkins & Associates, Inc. THORNTON, LALIA MITCHELL. "Confession" from *The Saturday Evening Post* magazine, September 14, 1929. Used by permission of The Saturday Evening Post Society. Our sincere thanks to the following authors or their heirs, some of whom we were unable to locate: Georgia B. Adams, Jessie Goddard Broman, Joyce E. Driver, Caroline Darr Fitzsimmons, Loise Pinkerton Fritz, Gretchen Gerhard, Sudie Stuart Hager, Alma Robison Higbee, Kari Sharp Hill, Starlette Howard, Barbara A. Jones, James Keller, Pamela Kennedy, Thelma Scott Kiser, Katherine Edelman Lyon, Marcella Drennan Malarky, Alice Leedy Mason, Virginia Scott Miner, Mrs. Roy L. Peifer, Marilyn Pribus, Edna Moore Schultz, Anne Campbell Stark, Laura W. Stevens, Delphia Stubbs, Georgia Sykes Sullivan, Lucile Waer, Grace V. Watkins, Johanna Ter Wee.